W9-BGY-195

Spirit & Truth

A self-guided Scripture study for confirmation and beyond

A CANDIDATE RESOURCE

Given to _____

by _____

In the year of Our Lord _____

Spirit
& Truth

A Self-Guided Scripture Study
for Confirmation and Beyond

A Candidate Resource

MICHAEL CAROTTA

TWENTY-THIRD PUBLICATIONS
A Division of Bayard
One Montauk Avenue, Suite 200
New London, CT 06320
(860) 437-3012 or (800) 321-0411
www.23rdpublications.com

Copyright ©2011 Michael Carotta. All rights reserved. No part of this publication may be reproduced in any manner without prior written permission of the publisher. Write to the Permissions Editor.

Scripture quotations in this work are based upon the *New American Bible with Revised New Testament and Revised Psalms*.

All catechism quotations from *Catechism of the Catholic Church*, Second Edition.

ISBN 978-1-58595-839-9
Library of Congress Catalog Card Number: 2011927378

Printed in the U.S.A.

CONTENTS

Recall then that you have received the spiritual seal, the spirit of wisdom and understanding, the spirit of right judgment and courage, the spirit of knowledge and reverence, the spirit of holy fear in God's presence.

Guard what you have received.

God the Father has marked you with his sign; Christ the Lord has confirmed you and has placed his pledge, the Spirit, in your hearts.

▶ SAINT AMBROSE

The Breath of God...

A mother, giving birth in a hospital delivery room, squeezes her husband's hand as her newborn arrives; she anxiously waits to hear the baby take its first *breath*.

A coach calls a timeout so a team of exhausted players can catch their *breath*.

A family gathers around their elderly parent's bedside, joining hands and praying, watching their loved one take the very last *breath*.

Breath is the invisible energy that brings and sustains life. The Holy Spirit is the Breath of God. It's what God gives us to sustain our spiritual life.

How much do you actually know about the Spirit?

In what ways has the Spirit influenced you and your life?

What can you do to increase your relationship with the Spirit?

Life in the Spirit is at the heart of what the Church celebrates in confirmation.

This study journal is a small part of your preparation. Centered on the Spirit, it can help you...

- learn what the Bible and the Catholic Church say about the Holy Spirit

- look more deeply at your past experiences to discover how the Spirit moves within you

- strengthen your prayer life

- increase your capacity to *sense the Spirit* and benefit from it

According to a recent survey by National Study of Youth and Religion, fifty percent of Catholic young people say they never read the Bible. This journal will take you through passages about the Holy Spirit from both the Old and New Testament. The reflection questions will help you revisit your past encounters with the Spirit and help you make sense of what's ahead—beyond confirmation.

Prayer is a big part of this journal. You will find space to write a short prayer after each Scripture passage. You can also learn what the Church teaches by reading the quotes from the *Catechism of the Catholic Church*, which are spread throughout. (Note: If you want a more complete presentation of the Catholic view of the Holy Spirit, see the *Catechism of the Catholic Church*. Begin with paragraphs #683–810.)

You can work through this self-study at your own pace and in your own place. Here's all you have to do:

Read. Each Scripture passage reveals something unique about the Holy Spirit. Read each one slowly so the words sink in.

Personalize it. The questions will help you jot down what you have personally found to be true about the Spirit's work in your life. That's why this journal is called *Spirit and Truth*.

Pray. Write a brief prayer that reflects what you're feeling or thinking. To best express yourself, think about TAPP. A TAPP prayer includes some or all of the following:

Thanksgiving

Admitting your mistakes

Pausing and listening to the Spirit's voice

Petitioning for your needs and the needs of others

The "See What You Think" word plays can help you see things from different angles and make new connections:

REMEM**BE**R
true self

See the word "be" in "remember"? The "true self" beneath it is a clue. It might remind you to "be who you really are." You might see something else—there's no right or wrong answer. Keep an open mind and jot down your thoughts. Date your responses and return later, as often as you want. You may see something different next time.

I believe in the Holy Spirit, the Lord, the giver of life, who proceeds from the Father and the Son, who with the Father and the Son is adored and glorified, who has spoken through the prophets.

▶ **FROM THE NICENE CREED**

What the **Bible** says about the **Holy Spirit**

— FORTY FOR NOW —

The first forty Scripture passages and questions in this journal can help you prepare for confirmation. The next forty are for life after confirmation. Think of your journaling as your "me" time—the time you spend getting to truly recognize the Spirit in your life. These are also your "notes to self." You will never be asked to share them with others. If you want to extend that "me time," feel free to look up the Scripture and catechism quotations to learn more.

[1]

Teach me to do your will, for you are my God. May your kind spirit lead me on a level path.   » PSALM 143:10

○ What kind of path have I been on in my life?

○ Is the Spirit trying to lead me on a level path? If so, what is it?

○ My prayer…

▓ The Church teaches…

The Holy Spirit is a gentle guest and friend, who inspires, guides, corrects, and strengthens—the interior Master of life according to Christ. (CCC 1697)

[2]

There are different kinds of spiritual gifts but the same spirit; there are different forms of service but the same Lord; there are different workings but the same God who produces all of them in everyone. To each individual the manifestation of the Spirit is given for some benefit.   » 1 CORINTHIANS 12:4–7

◐ The Spirit improves the way people do their work. When and how has the Spirit enhanced the work I do—school...sports...music... art?

◉ The Spirit gives us all different gifts so we can help others. What are my gifts?

◐ How do I know these gifts are from God?

◐ My prayer...

[3]

Even on the servants and the handmaids, in those days, I will pour out my spirit. » JOEL 3:2

For in one Spirit we were all baptized into one body—Jews and Greeks, slaves or free—and we were all given to drink of one Spirit. » 1 CORINTHIANS 12:13

For your imperishable spirit is in all things. » WISDOM 12:1

⟳ God pours the Spirit on all people, not just some. What groups of people do I need to remember are blessed with the Spirit?

⟳ What does this say to me about how God designed the human race?

⟳ My prayer...

■ **See What You Think...** ⋯⋯⋯⋯⋯⋯⋯⋯⋯⋯⋯⋯⋯⋯⋯⋯

M Y S T E R Y
on your mind

[4]

Let every creature serve you, for you spoke and they were made. You sent forth your spirit and they were created: no one can resist your word. » JUDITH 16:14

◉ God the Father created everything through the Spirit. All can hear the Spirit's voice. When the Spirit speaks to me, is it more like a whisper, a feeling in my stomach, a persistent reminder, or a push from behind?

◉ My prayer…

▮ The Church teaches…

As Christians, we are temples of the Holy Spirit. All humans are blessed with a spiritual and immortal soul and can participate in the light and power of the divine Spirit. Our souls and minds can:

- *seek and love what is true and good*
- *recognize the voice of God urging us to toward good and away from evil*
- *understand the order of things established by the Creator* (CCC 1703-06)

[5]

Now this is how the birth of Jesus Christ came about. When his mother Mary was betrothed to Joseph, but before they lived together, she was found with child through the Holy Spirit....The angel of the Lord appeared to Joseph in a dream and said, "Joseph, son of David, do not be afraid to take Mary your wife into your home. For it is through the Holy Spirit that this child has been conceived in her." » MATTHEW 1:18, 20

The angel said to her: "The Holy Spirit will come upon you, and the power of the Most High will overshadow you; therefore the child to be born will be called holy, the Son of God."

» LUKE 1:35

○ The Holy Spirit has always been involved in spiritual and physical creation. What has the Holy Spirit created in my life? Was it physical or spiritual?

○ My prayer...

■ See What You Think...

YOUR

where's the tension?

[6]

But the Spirit of the Lord came upon Samson, and he tore
the lion in pieces as one might tear apart a kid goat. However
he did not mention to his father or mother what he had done.

» JUDGES 14:6–7

● When has the Spirit helped me do something strong or courageous
that I didn't want to tell my parents about?

● My prayer…

● **See What You Think...**

THRILL

agree? if so, when? how?

[7]

The Spirit of God rushed upon Saul and he became very
angry. » 1 SAMUEL 11:6

○ Sometimes the Spirit leads a person to righteous anger, like the
time Jesus overturned the moneychangers' tables. Jesus knew these
people were taking advantage of the poor who were trying to pray
in the temple. When have I experienced the Spirit fueling my righteous anger?

○ Did I accomplish anything with it?

○ When have I seen righteous anger expressed by someone else?

○ What righteous anger might the Spirit be asking me to express these days?

○ When have I seen or used righteous anger as an excuse for unjustifiable anger?

○ My prayer...

[8]

Create a clean heart for me, God; renew in me a steadfast spirit. » PSALM 51:12

The Spirit cleanses. What do I want the Spirit to cleanse in me?

How hard am I working on it?

My prayer...

The Church teaches...

The Holy Spirit renews us internally through spiritual transformation, and enlightens and strengthens us to live as children of the light through all that is good and right and true. The Holy Spirit heals wounds caused by sin.
(CCC 1695)

[9]

For the spirit of God has made me, and the breath of the Almighty gives me life. » JOB 33:4

○ I certainly can't remember my first breath. But my mom or my dad might. Maybe I can ask them about it if they're around. Notes:

○ Do I know anyone who's witnessed a loved one give up the final breath? Maybe I can ask them about it. Notes:

○ What does it all say to me about the connection between the Spirit and life itself?

○ What in this Scripture do I need to remember most?

○ My prayer...

[10]

And do not grieve the Holy Spirit of God, with which you were sealed for the day of redemption. » EPHESIANS 4:30

Whoever speaks a word against the Son of Man will be forgiven, but whoever speaks against the Holy Spirit will not be forgiven, either in this age or in the age to come.

» MATTHEW 12:32

Whoever blasphemes against the Holy Spirit will never have forgiveness, but is guilty of everlasting sin. » MARK 3:29

○ These verses refer to the seal of confirmation and about choosing the unholy over the holy. What forms can the unholy take?

○ What have I come to recognize as evil, that is, against the ways of God?

○ My prayer…

See What You Think…

N O N E
won't tolerate…

[11]

I am full of words; the spirit within me constrains me.

» JOB 32:18

○ When has the Holy Spirit helped me control my emotions and hold my tongue?

○ When have I felt the Spirit's constraint but ignored it, allowing my emotions to rule?

○ My prayer…

■ **See What You Think…**

N**ONE**

who stood up

[12]

For those who are led by the Spirit of God are children of God. » ROMANS 8:14

O How do I know when I meet someone who's led by the Spirit? How do they act?

O If the Spirit makes us all related as children of God, how should I be treating others?

O What about the person I'm going out with? The person I used to go out with? The person I want to go out with?

O My prayer...

▧ The Church teaches...

The Holy Spirit, the Third Person of the Trinity, was at work with the Father and the Son helping shape Creation. The Spirit is "principal author" of the Scriptures. And the Virgin Mary conceived Christ through the Holy Spirit. (CCC 685, 689, 703, 695, 304, 723)

[13]

Jesus came and stood in their midst and said to them, "Peace be with you." When he had said this, he showed them his hands and his side. The disciples rejoiced when they saw the Lord. Jesus said to them again, "Peace be with you. As the Father has sent me, so I send you." And when he had said this, he breathed on them and said to them, "Receive the Holy Spirit."   » JOHN 20:19–22

o The Spirit came to them as the Breath of God. The old Hebrew word for that is *ruah*. Jesus emphasized that the Spirit brings peace. What do I need spiritual peace over right now?

o My prayer…

See What You Think…

s I N

what's popular?

[14]

The Spirit entered into me and set me on my feet and he spoke with me. He said to me: "Go; shut yourself in your house."

» EZEKIEL 3:24

Like cattle going down into the plain, the Spirit of the Lord gave them rest. » ISAIAH 63:14

- The Spirit often urges us to get rest and find some solitude. Where does the Spirit give me a place of rest? Is it a physical or mental place?

- What's restful about it?

- How comfortable am I with the practice of solitude? What spiritual benefits have I found in solitude?

- My prayer…

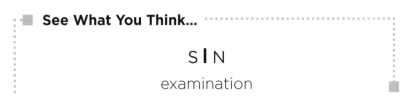

See What You Think…

S I N

examination

[15]

Jesus answered, "Amen, amen, I say to you, no one can enter the kingdom of God without being born of water and Spirit."

» JOHN 3:5

○ Baptism and confirmation are sacraments that connect physical birth with our spiritual re-birth. In what way have I experienced a spiritual re-birth, or a time when I remembered and returned to the kind of spiritual person I have always wanted to be?

○ My prayer...

▪ **See What You Think...**

REMEMBER
in what way?

[16]

So long as I still have life in me and the breath of God is in my nostrils… » JOB 27:3

○ Here's how I can finish this sentence to say what's most important to me:

○ My prayer…

Gen 2:7 The Lord God formed a (person) out of the clay of the ground & blew into his nostrils the breath of life, & so man became a living being.

▨ The Church teaches…

The term "Spirit" translates from the Hebrew word **ruah**, *which means breath, air, wind. The first two lines of the Bible tell us that the earth was created with a mighty wind, literally translated "a wind, breath of God" and "spirit of God" (Genesis 1:1–2). And Jesus, after his death and resurrection, appeared to the Apostles. He "breathed on them and said, 'Receive the Holy Spirit.'"* (JOHN 20:22; CCC 691, 730)

[17]

Therefore I prayed, and understanding was given to me; I called on God, and the Spirit of wisdom came to me...for wisdom, the fashioner of all things, taught me. For in her is a spirit intelligent, holy, unique, manifold, subtle, agile, clear, unstained, certain, not baneful, loving the good, keen, unhampered, beneficent, kindly... » WISDOM 7:7, 22–23

○ Wisdom is often referred to as female. The Spirit brings true Wisdom, and the Bible says this about the Spirit more than anything else. What Wisdom has the Spirit brought to me?

○ What exactly have I done to receive the Spirit's Wisdom?

○ What wisdom am I seeking now?

○ My prayer...

[18]

Then Samuel, with the horn of oil in hand, anointed him in the midst of his brothers, and from that day on, the Spirit of the Lord rushed upon David.   » 1 SAMUEL 16:13

Now when the apostles in Jerusalem heard that Samaria had accepted the word of God, they sent them Peter and John, who went down and prayed for them, that they might receive the Holy Spirit, for it had not yet fallen upon any of them; they had only been baptized in the name of the Lord Jesus. Then they laid hands on them and they received the Holy Spirit.

» ACTS 8:14–17

○ This sounds like what's going to happen at confirmation. What does God expect of me personally after confirmation?

○ What new spiritual responsibilities come with my anointing?

○ My prayer...

See What You Think...

BELIEVE
make a list

[19]

If you love me, you will keep my commandments. And I
will ask the Father and he will give you another Advocate
to be with you always, the Spirit of truth, which the world
cannot accept, because it neither sees nor knows it. But you
know it, because it remains with you, and will be in you.

» JOHN 14:15–17

○ Jesus is saying five things here.
1. If we love him, we need to keep his commands.
2. The Spirit is the Advocate, the one who sticks up for us.
3. The Spirit always shows Truth.
4. The world has different interests and doesn't recognize the ways
of the Spirit very well.
5. We can recognize the Spirit because the Spirit lives in each of us.

Of these five, the ones the Spirit wants me to remember most these
days are:

○ My prayer…

See What You Think…

BELIEF

name some

[20]

The spirit of the Lord spoke through me, his word was on my tongue. » 2 SAMUEL 23:2

○ When has the Spirit told me what to say and how to say it?

○ When have I felt someone was speaking to me with words from the Spirit?

○ My prayer…

■ The Church teaches…

"Holy Spirit" is the proper name for the Third Person of the Trinity, which is different but inseparable from God the Father and God the Son. It is the name used most often in the Acts of the Apostles and the Epistles. Jesus called the Spirit the Paraclete, literally "he who is called to one's side." Paraclete is also translated to mean "consoler" and "advocate." The Lord also called the Holy Spirit "the Spirit of truth." (JOHN 14:16, 26; 15:26; 16:7, 13; CCC 689, 692)

[21]

When the time for Pentecost was fulfilled, they were all in one place together. And suddenly there came from the sky a noise like a strong driving wind, and it filled the entire house in which they were. Then there appeared to them tongues as of fire, which parted and came to rest on each one of them. And they were all filled with the Holy Spirit and began to speak in different tongues, as the Spirit enabled them to proclaim.

Now there were devout Jews from every nation under heaven staying in Jerusalem. At this sound, they gathered in a large crowd, but they were confused because each one heard them speaking in his own language....They were all astounded and bewildered, and said to one another, "What does this mean?" But others said, scoffing, "They have had too much new wine." » ACTS 2:1–6, 12–13

○ The Spirit speaks a universal language that each person can hear within his or her own soul. What messages from the Spirit do I believe all people universally hear and accept, no matter what language they speak?

○ My prayer...

■ Pencil it in...

Christmas celebrates the arrival of Christ. Pentecost is the public coming of the Holy Spirit to all mankind. Find out which Sunday the Church celebrates Pentecost this year. Mark it down and come to Mass as your own way of giving the Spirit praise.

[22]

The hand of the Lord came upon me, and he led me out in the spirit of the Lord and set me in the center of the plain, which was filled with bones. » EZEKIEL 37:1

○ When has the Spirit shown me the "dead bones" of a situation—the ugly truth?

○ What truth did I see? What did I do about it?

○ My prayer...

[23]

When they lead you away and hand you over, do not worry beforehand about what you are to say. But say whatever will be given to you at that hour. For it will not be you who are speaking but the Holy Spirit. » MARK 13:11

○ When has the Spirit given me the words I need to defend myself?

○ Do I need any today? If so, about what?

○ My prayer…

See What You Think…

K N O W

discovering

[24]

The Advocate, the Holy Spirit that the Father will send in my name—he will teach you everything and remind you of all that I told you. » JOHN 14:26

◓ What are some things I've learned with the Holy Spirit's help?

◓ What has the Holy Spirit written on my heart, or reminded me about?

◓ My prayer…

✷✸✺

▉ The Church teaches... ·········

And the Spirit still comes into the world without ever stopping…continuing to animate all mankind…revealing God…awakening faith, and enabling communication with Christ. (CCC 732, 687, 684, 683)

The Spirit is the source of all holiness, restoring us, helping us grow in spiritual freedom, and granting spiritual gifts to all. (CCC 749, 733, 1742, 2003)

[25]

I will put my spirit within you, and make you live by my statutes, careful to observe my decrees. » EZEKIEL 36:27

○ The Spirit gives us the grace to follow God's laws. Which of God's laws do I need the Spirit's help with?

○ How careful am I about following God's law?

○ My prayer...

The Church teaches...

Confirmation increases the gifts of the Holy Spirit in us. Like baptism, it is given only once, because it too imprints on the soul an indelible spiritual mark—the seal of the Spirit, which unites us more firmly to Christ and to his Body, the Church. (CCC 1303-04)

[26]

One of them named Agabus stood up and predicted by the Spirit that there would be a severe famine over all the world, and it happened under Claudius.   » ACTS 11:28

○ When has the Spirit tried to warn me about something, or shown me something that was coming?

○ When have I ignored a warning from the Spirit and said something like, "I knew this was going to happen, I just knew it!" Could that have been the Spirit warning me? What happened next?

○ My prayer…

See What You Think...

LIFE
luck? fate? what?

[27]

Make no mistake: God is not mocked, for a person will reap only what he sows, because the one who sows for his flesh will reap corruption from the flesh. But the one who sows for the Spirit will reap eternal life from the Spirit. Let us not grow tired of doing good, for in due time we shall reap our harvest.

» GALATIANS 6:7–9

○ An important Spirit law: We harvest what we plant. We get back what we dish out. What do I wish I could change about past actions or interactions?

○ What do I wish I could stop doing?

○ What do I wish I could start doing more often?

○ My prayer...

See What You Think...

WISDOM
what insights?

[28]

After Jesus was baptized, he came up from the water, and suddenly the heavens were opened for him and he saw the Spirit of God descending like a dove and coming upon him. And a voice came from the heavens, saying, "This is my beloved Son, with whom I am well pleased." » MATTHEW 3:16–17

○ At Jesus' baptism the Spirit took the form of a dove. I'd have to say that at different times in my life, the Spirit has taken different forms. For example:

○ God said he was "well pleased" with Jesus. Here's what I think the Spirit would say is true about me:

○ My prayer…

See What You Think…

WISDOM

what actions?

[29]

This is the pact that I made with you when you came out of Egypt, and my Spirit continues in your midst; do not fear.

» HAGGAI 2:5

For God did not give us a spirit of fear, but rather a spirit of power and love and self-control. » 2 TIMOTHY 1:7

○ The Spirit was part of the Promise and helps us overcome fear. Which of these fears concern me? (Circle.)

fear of rejection   fear of failure   fear of pain   fear of loss

○ The Spirit brings power, love, and self-discipline. Which of these gifts do I want and need most these days? (Circle.)

power   love   self-discipline

○ My prayer…

See What You Think…

ADMIT

what?

[30]

As Peter was pondering the vision, the Spirit said to him, "There are three men here looking for you. So get up, go downstairs, and accompany them without hesitation, because I have sent them." » ACTS 10:19–20

○ The Spirit lets us know when we should do something, and with whom. When was the last time this happened to me?

○ What did I learn?

○ My prayer…

■ **The Church teaches...**

The symbols of the Holy Spirit:

water: *new birth experienced in baptism; the ongoing source of nourishment for the soul*

oil: *called and blessed by God; used in anointing*

fire: *spiritual energy, passion, and determination that come from the Spirit*

cloud, light: *guidance, direction, and spiritual insights*

seal: *permanent decision or commitment; a mark of identification*

hand: *the Spirit's healing touch and protection*

finger: *the Spirit's power to create ("written by the finger of God")*

dove: *the Spirit's ability to bring peace, comfort, and confidence* (CCC 691-701, 730)

While they were worshiping the Lord and fasting, the Holy Spirit said, "Set apart for me Barnabas and Saul for the work to which I called them."…So they, sent forth by the Holy Spirit, went down to Seleucia, and from there sailed to Cyprus.

» ACTS 13:2, 4

So the Twelve called together the community of disciples and said, "It is not right for us to neglect the word of God to serve at table. Brothers, select from among you seven reputable men, filled with the Spirit and wisdom, whom we shall appoint to this task, whereas we shall devote ourselves to prayer and to the ministry of the word." » ACTS 6:2–4

○ The Spirit has always helped the Church decide who does what. Now that I am being confirmed, what contribution is the Spirit asking me to make to the Church?

○ What's it going to cost?

○ My prayer…

[32]

But as for me, I am filled with power, with the spirit of the Lord, with authority and with might; to declare to Jacob his crimes and to Israel his sins. » MICAH 3:8

○ The Spirit brings inner strength to help us stand up for justice. When have I known that the Spirit was urging me to confront someone's wrongdoing?

○ What, if anything, is the Spirit asking me to stand up for today?

○ My prayer…

▪ The Church teaches…

First and foremost, the Holy Spirit brings us the gift of God's love. God's love has been poured into our hearts through the Holy Spirit that has been given to us. (ROMANS 5:5)

The Spirit also brings us the gifts of wisdom, understanding, counsel, fortitude, knowledge, piety, and fear of the Lord. The purpose of all the Spirit's gifts is to help us live the virtues. (CCC 733, 1830-31)

[33]

I will pour out my spirit on all mankind; your sons and daugh-
ters shall prophesy, your old men shall dream dreams, your
young men shall see visions.   » JOEL 3:1

○ The Spirit helps us see what is possible for our lives and what God
has in mind for us. What Dream has the Spirit put in my heart?

○ What little dreams make up the big Dream that my soul holds
dear?

○ My prayer…

See What You Think…

CH**U**RCH
how's it going?

[34]

Do not get drunk on wine, in which lies debauchery; but be filled with the spirit.   » EPHESIANS 5:18

○ There's a difference between feeling high and feeling good. One comes from spirits, the other from the Spirit. I think the Bible makes this statement because God...

○ I think the wisdom here is:

○ My prayer...

See What You Think...

ARGUMENTS
who? about?

[35]

The Spirit comes to the aid of our weakness, for we do not know how to pray as we ought, but the Spirit itself intercedes for us with sighs too deep for words. And the one who searches hearts, knows what is the mind of the Spirit, because the Spirit intercedes for the holy ones according to God's will.

» ROMANS 8:26–27

○ The Spirit intercedes for us. That's what an advocate does, especially when we can't seem to find the words. Here's a seven-word prayer to the Spirit that I'm willing to create, memorize, and use whenever I'm at a loss of words or just want to check in:

See What You Think...

```
          A
          W
          A
          K
C O N V E R S I O N
          N
          I
          N
          G
      need most
```

[36]

Live by the Spirit and you will certainly not gratify the desires of the flesh. For the flesh has desires against the Spirit; and the Spirit against the flesh; these are opposed to each other, so that you may not do what you want...Now the works of the flesh are obvious: immorality, impurity, licentiousness, idolatry, sorcery, hatreds, rivalry, jealousy, outbursts of fury, acts of selfishness, dissensions, factions, occasions of envy, drinking bouts, orgies, and the like.

I warn you, as I have warned you before, that those who do such things will not inherit the kingdom of God.

In contrast, the fruit of the Spirit is love, joy, peace, patience, kindness, generosity, faithfulness, gentleness, self-control. » GALATIANS 5:16–17, 19–23

○ When has the Spirit told me I was going downhill, or the wrong way?

○ How well did I change direction?

○ The Spirit looks for treasures beyond, above and deeper than the physical. How much do I look for treasures that are way beyond the physical?

○ What worries me most about life in the Spirit?

○ What's the hardest part?

○ My prayer…

[37]

Do you not know that your body is a temple of the Holy Spirit within you, whom you have from God, and that you are not your own? » 1 CORINTHIANS 6:19

⊙ Spiritually speaking, I need to remember who I am and to whom I really belong. Here's a list of three things I need to do to get better at honoring my body:

1.

2.

3.

⊙ Here are some ways I can get better at honoring the bodies of others:

1.

2.

3.

⊙ My prayer…

[38]

There is one body and one Spirit, just as you were called to the one hope of your call. » EPHESIANS 4:4

○ What might the Spirit be showing me about my call?

○ What's my spiritual Promise? What kind of person am I to become?

○ My prayer…

■ The Church teaches…

Today, the grace of the Holy Spirit has the power to help us with the process of ongoing conversion, our continuing turning toward God the Father and to all that is good and right and true.

This is accomplished by daily gestures of reconciliation, concern for the poor, the exercise and defense of justice, admission of our faults, acceptance of correction, revising our life, examination of conscience, spiritual direction, acceptance of suffering and persecution, and following Christ. (CCC 2017, 1695, 1435)

[39]

Do not quench the Spirit. » 1 THESSALONIANS 5:19

○ What common actions or interactions can quench the Spirit?

○ What happens if someone does quench the Spirit?

○ My prayer…

◼ The Church teaches…

What the soul is to the human body, the Holy Spirit is to the Body of Christ, the Church. Just as the human body is a temple of the Holy Spirit, the Church, as the mystical Body of Christ, is also a temple of the Holy Spirit. Since Pentecost, it is the place where we know the Holy Spirit. (CCC 797-8, 731, 688)

The Spirit directs and unifies the Church. The Spirit is present in the Church's liturgy, sacraments, and prayer. It is the Holy Spirit that guides and shapes the teaching and Tradition of the Church. And it is the Spirit that fuels the Church's mission.

By your confirmation, you are now a fully initiated member of this Church. (CCC 768, 747, 813, 1091-1109, 737, 739, 852)

[40]

May the God of hope fill you with all joy and peace in believing, so that you may abound in hope by the power of the Holy Spirit.   » ROMANS 15:13

○ The Spirit always brings hope. And hope brings joy. What causes me to lose hope sometimes?

○ When have I experienced the Spirit bringing me hope?

○ How can I maintain my hope?

○ What do I need from the Spirit to help me stay hopeful?

○ My prayer...

See What You Think...

PROBLEM
talk to...

The Old Testament proclaimed the Father clearly but the Son more obscurely. The New Testament revealed the Son and gave us a glimpse of the divinity of the Spirit. Now the Spirit dwells among us and grants us a clearer vision of himself.

► CATECHISM OF THE CATHOLIC CHURCH

What the **Bible** says about the **Holy Spirit**

Although the following pages are designed to help deepen your knowledge and experience of the Spirit after you've been confirmed, don't feel like you have to wait to work on this portion. That's only a guideline. If you need more room, feel free to extend your journaling to a notebook or other format. Whatever works for you.

[1]

Now the Lord is the Spirit, and where the Spirit of the Lord is, there is freedom.   » 2 CORINTHIANS 3:17

○ The Spirit brings me freedom from:

○ The Spirit gives me freedom to:

[2]

The disciples were filled with joy and the Holy Spirit.

» ACTS 13:52

○ The Spirit actually does bring joy, which is deeper, different from enthusiasm. What brings me spiritual joy?

○ How do I know when I have joy, as opposed to just feeling good?

[3]

They failed to know who formed them, and breathed into them
a quickening soul, and infused a vital spirit. » WISDOM 15:11

○ What causes people to "fail to know"?

[4]

Keep watch over yourselves and over all the flock, of which the
Holy Spirit has made you overseers, to shepherd the church
of God that he obtained with the blood of his own Son.

» ACTS 20:28

○ God intended to establish a church and that the Spirit accompany
those appointed to oversee and shepherd its members. How would
I describe my relationship with the Catholic Church?

[5]

The grace of the Lord Jesus Christ, the love of God, and the fellowship of the Holy Spirit be with all of you.

» 2 CORINTHIANS 13:13

● Another reminder of the Trinity. What does "fellowship of the Holy Spirit" mean to me?

[6]

The only thing I want to learn from you is this: Did you receive the Spirit by doing works of the law or by believing what you heard? » GALATIANS 3:2

● Great question. And what would I say?

[7]

The spirit lifted me up, and brought me into the inner court;
and I saw the temple was filled with the glory of the Lord.

» EZEKIEL 43:5

○ Prayer can take us to the "inner court" and let us sense the glory of
God. What can I do to deepen my prayer life so I can get into the
inner court?

○ Has my prayer ever taken me there? What was it like?

[8]

For I know that this will result in deliverance for me through
your prayers and support from the Spirit of Jesus Christ.

» PHILIPPIANS 1:19

○ Two powers are at work here. Who can I ask to pray for me?

○ And whom can I pray for?

[9]

They went through the Phrygian and Galatian territory because they had been prevented by the Holy Spirit from preaching the message in Asia.   » ACTS 16:6

○ Sometimes the Spirit wants me to hold my tongue—even if I'm right. When have I felt the Spirit urging me to hold my tongue?

○ How'd that go for me?

[10]

I baptize you with water for repentance, but one who is coming after me is mightier than I. I am not worthy to carry his sandals. He will baptize you with the Holy Spirit and fire.

» MATTHEW 3:11

○ John the Baptist, foretelling of Christ, connected the Holy Spirit with fire. Why is fire associated with the Holy Spirit?

○ When have I experienced or used this kind of fire?

[11]

The Spirit of God is upon me, because the Lord has anointed me; he has sent me to bring glad tidings to the lowly, to heal the brokenhearted, to proclaim liberty to the captives, and release to the prisoners. » ISAIAH 61:1

O What has the Spirit anointed you to do?

O Come up with four you are willing to devote yourself to.

[12]

Go therefore and make disciples of all nations, baptizing them in the name of the Father and of the Son and of the Holy Spirit. » MATTHEW 28:19

O Jesus' command indicates the importance of the Trinity. We remind ourselves of this with the Sign of the Cross. Why do I use it?

O When should I use it more often?

[13]

But the spirit of the Lord enveloped Gideon, and he blew the horn that summoned Abiezer to follow him. » JUDGES 6:34

○ When have I been inspired as a leader, or been led by someone inspired?

○ How could I tell? What was it like?

[14]

Where can I hide from your spirit? Where can I flee from your presence? » PSALM 139:7

○ We are made to be drawn to the Spirit. I can make two more questions/statements like those in this psalm:

1.

2.

[15]

Then the spirit of God took possession of Zechariah, son of the priest Jehoiada; he stood above the people and said to them, "God says, 'Why are you transgressing the Lord's commands?'" » 2 CHRONICLES 24:20

○ The Spirit sometimes compels us to ask challenging questions. When has this happened to me? What question was I led to ask?

○ When has the Spirit used someone else to ask me a challenging question?

[16]

Do not drive me from your presence, and do not take your holy Spirit from me. » PSALM 51:13

○ Lose the Comforter, the Advocate, and we lose peace and direction. When have I felt despair or been disheartened?

○ How did I find the Spirit to recover? Or have I yet to find it?

○ What advice can I give someone else feeling this kind of loss?

---

[17]

Who has learned your counsel, unless you have given wisdom and sent your holy Spirit from on high? » WISDOM 9:17

○ We can only learn God's will through the Spirit. What do I need the Spirit's wisdom for these days?

---

[18]

Here is my servant, whom I uphold, my chosen one, with whom I am pleased; I have put my spirit upon him; he will bring forth justice to the nations. » ISAIAH 42:1

○ How would I rate myself as a servant of God?

○ What is the Spirit asking me to "bring forth"?

[19]

If you then, who are wicked, know how to give good gifts to your children, how much more will the Father in heaven give the Holy Spirit to those who ask him? » LUKE 11:13

◉ I'd like to ask the Spirit for:

[20]

"Could we find another like him," Pharaoh asked his officials, "a man so endowed with the spirit of God?" » GENESIS 41:38

◉ Here are two people I know "in whom is the spirit of God":

[21]

But you will receive power when the Holy Spirit comes upon you; and you will be my witnesses in Jerusalem, throughout Judea and Samaria, and to the ends of the earth. » ACTS 1:8

○ How can someone witness or be a witness of Christ?

○ What kind of power do we need?

○ How is the Spirit inviting me to be a witness? And what kind of power do I need?

[22]

Peter said to them, "Repent, and be baptized, every one of you, in the name of Jesus Christ for the forgiveness of your sins; and you will receive the gift of the Holy Spirit."

» ACTS 2:38

○ Repentance helps open us up to the experience of the Spirit. What is tugging on my heart, urging me to repent and ask God for forgiveness? To help bring it forward, I'll just use a word, initial, or symbol here.

[23]

The spirit of the Lord shall rest on him, a spirit of wisdom and understanding, a spirit of counsel and strength, a spirit of knowledge and fear of the Lord. » ISAIAH 11:2

○ Which one of these do I need and want most these days? (Circle one above.)

[24]

If the Spirit of him who raised Jesus from the dead dwells in you, he who raised Christ from the dead will give life to your mortal bodies also through his Spirit that dwells in you.
» ROMANS 8:11

○ What questions do I still have about life after life?

○ Who can I discuss them with?

[25]

I speak the truth in Christ—I do not lie; my conscience joins with the Holy Spirit. » ROMANS 9:1

- How much of my conscience do I think the Holy Spirit would confirm as correct?

- When have I followed my conscience even though it cost me?

- When have I ignored my conscience and didn't follow the Spirit's voice?

[26]

Now there was a man in Jerusalem whose name was Simeon. This man was righteous and devout, awaiting the consolation of Israel, and the Holy Spirit was on him. It had been revealed to him by the Holy Spirit that he should not see death before he had seen the Lord's Messiah. » LUKE 2:25–26

- The Spirit reveals things to righteous people. What has the Spirit revealed to me?

[27]

To set the mind on the flesh is death, but to set the mind on the Spirit is life and peace.   » ROMANS 8:6

◖ What am I setting my mind on, exactly?

[28]

God is Spirit and those who worship him must worship in Spirit and truth.   » JOHN 4: 24

◖ To me, worshiping well means…

[29]

He who has prepared us for this very thing is God, who has given us the Spirit as a guarantee. » 2 CORINTHIANS 5:5

○ I think the "thing" St. Paul is talking about is:

○ I think the Spirit guarantees:

[30]

Guard the good treasure entrusted to you, with the help of the Holy Spirit dwelling in us. » 2 TIMOTHY 1:14

○ What treasure was entrusted to me?

○ How can I guard it, and why should I? What can happen to it?

[31]

The spirit lifted me up and brought me in a vision by the spirit of God into Chaldea, to the exiles. Then the vision that I had seen left me. » EZEKIEL 11:24

○ The Spirit helps me glimpse what's possible for my life, what God has in mind for me, or the role that best matches up with my soul. Which of these has the Spirit helped me see recently?

[32]

Then the Spirit of the Lord fell upon me, and he told me to say: "Thus says the Lord: This is the way you talk, house of Israel, and what you are plotting I well know." » EZEKIEL 11:5

For the Spirit of the Lord fills the world, is all-embracing and knows what man says. » WISDOM 1:7

○ The Spirit knows my deepest thoughts. Here are some I really want to put on the table:

[33]

No one knows what pertains to God except the Spirit of God. We have not received the spirit of the world but the Spirit that is from God....And we speak about them not with words taught by human wisdom, but with words taught by the Spirit, describing spiritual realities in spiritual terms.

» 1 CORINTHIANS 2:11–13

○ The Spirit speaks a language of the soul and may or may not use words spoken or written by humans. What advice can I offer someone who wants to learn the language of the Spirit?

[34]

If we live by the Spirit let us also be guided by the Spirit. Let us not be conceited, provoking one another, envious of one another. » GALATIANS 5:25–26

○ I'll add three more qualities to that. "Let us be

_____, _____,

and _____."

[35]

My friends, even if a person is caught in some transgression, you who are spiritual should correct that one in a spirit of gentleness. Look to yourself, so that you also may not be tempted.

» GALATIANS 6:1

⊙ The Spirit gives us tender strength and strong tenderness when it comes to confronting someone. But we are asked to be careful. Who or what might the Spirit be asking me to confront these days?

⊙ How can I do it "in a spirit of gentleness"?

[36]

Now the Spirit expressly says that in later times some will turn away from the faith by paying attention to deceitful spirits and teachings of demons. » 1 TIMOTHY 4:1

Beloved, do not trust every spirit but test the spirits to see whether they belong to God; because many false prophets have gone out into the world. » 1 JOHN 4:1

⊙ The unholy one is always about untruth, and is just as real as the Holy Spirit. How do I determine which is which?

○ When have I found myself following an untruth or the influence of the unholy?

○ How about now?

---

[37]

For God did not call us to impurity, but to holiness. Therefore whoever disregards this, disregards not a human being but God, who also gives his Holy Spirit to you.

» 1 THESSALONIANS 4:7–8

○ The Holy Spirit gives us the grace to increase our holiness. Seems obvious. How would I rate my level of holiness?

○ What can I do to increase it?

[38]

Take on the helmet of salvation, and the sword of the Spirit, which is the word of God. » EPHESIANS 6:17

○ What does this say about the connection between the Spirit and the Bible?

○ How can I find a way to read the Bible more often?

○ Why would the Spirit be described as a sword?

[39]

I kneel before the Father, from whom every family in heaven and on earth is named, that he may grant you in accord with the riches of his glory to be strengthened with power through his Spirit in the inner self. » EPHESIANS 3:14–16

○ The Spirit brings inner strength. What specific inner strength do I have?

[40]

But you, beloved, build yourselves up in your most holy faith;
pray in the Holy Spirit. » JUDE 1:20

Pray at every opportunity in the Spirit. To that end keep alert
and persevere. » EPHESIANS 6:18

○ Praying builds faith. How I can "build my faith"?

Growing
in the Spirit

Life in the Holy Spirit fulfills your vocation.
This life is made up of divine charity and
human solidarity. It is graciously offered as
salvation.

► CATECHISM OF THE CATHOLIC CHURCH #1699

There are many ways to keep growing in the Spirit. Most of them involve spiritual *practices*. Practices are behaviors or habits that help us open up to the Spirit while making each of us an instrument of the Spirit. Some spiritual practices involve attitudes and some require that we increase our knowledge. Practices help us keep in touch with the Spirit far beyond confirmation. Here are just a few. Pick one or two and begin making them your own.

Practicing Catholicism

Visit any city or country and you'll feel at home with practicing Catholics. Our built-in symbols and traditions—directly from Jesus and the Apostles—unite us in the Spirit.

We light candles to show how the Spirit helps us see in darkness. We use holy water to recall our baptism and life in the Spirit. The Sign of the Cross reminds us of God the Father, Son, and Holy Spirit.

We use colors. We have seasons. We fast. We kneel. We remember. We relive.

We celebrate the Eucharist as the Body of Christ and food for our journey.

For two thousand years, billions of Catholics have practiced their faith with its symbols, seasons, rituals, Scripture, and Tradition. It's how we sustain life in the Spirit.

> **?** What's your favorite Catholic symbol or season?
>
> **?** How has practicing your Catholicism helped you sense the Spirit?
>
> **?** What Catholic practices would you like to do more?

Fasting and prayer

This is a serious and ancient practice of denying ourselves something in order to sharpen our spiritual awareness or show spiritual support for someone else's situation. Its power lies in the sacrifice of denying ourselves something we enjoy. Some examples:

- Jesus is "led by the Spirit" into the wilderness where he fasts for forty days
- College students go on a hunger fast until an unfair practice is changed
- A teen notices her dad skips dessert. "On a diet?" she asks. "Nope," he responds, "gave it up until Uncle Gary finds a job."

When done responsibly and without dishonoring the body, the practice of fasting enhances prayer life. You can follow our Catholic tradition of lenten fast and sacrifice, or you can choose your own fast.

> **?** Jesus fasted before beginning his work. What's that say?

Virtues and moral imagination

A sophomore pictures herself as a person of integrity. A junior visualizes being a friend to the friendless. An athlete plays with sportsmanship. A person decides not to hook up. Another learns to control anger.

When you imagine yourself as a person "of the Way," standing "on the side of the angels," you move beyond being a believer and toward being a disciple. The Church identifies four cardinal, or foundational, virtues:

- **prudence:** correct reasoning
- **justice:** desire to uphold the rights and dignity of others
- **fortitude:** inner strength
- **temperance:** moderation and the ability to control desires

The Spirit empowers you with moral virtues like love, joy, peace, patience, kindness, generosity, faithfulness, gentleness, and self-control.

Jesus was all about moral imagination, calling us to discipleship: "You are the salt of the earth...Take the narrow road, not the wide one...Turn the other cheek...Walk not one mile but two...Whatever you do to those in need, you do to me."

> **?** What virtues will people use to describe you?
> **?** What situation(s) are moral challenges for you?

? What kind of spiritual person do you imagine yourself to be?

Bible study

Studying the Bible is like checking a compass for the right direction—the Way of God. God's word can console you when you're down, reminding you of the Spirit's presence, the Father's love, and the hope the Son brings.

You already know about the books of the Bible. But did you know that Roman Catholics use the Greek version of the Old Testament, containing forty-six books, while other Christians use the Hebrew version, with thirty-nine books?

Jesus said this about the Bible: "If you remain in my word, you will truly be my disciples, and you will know the truth. And the truth will set you free" (John 8:31–32). Pick one of the four gospels and read it. Make notes on what the Spirit shows you.

Discernment

"What do I do with my life? Does God have a plan for me?" A spiritual calling comes from another place and time—an invitation from God, encouragement from others, or the Spirit's gentle voice within.

Callings require spiritual listening called "discernment." We discern callings throughout life:

How am I to live as a child of God? (faith)

Who am I to live with? (relationships)

How am I to labor? (work)

Answers may not come quickly, and they're not always final. Sometimes worldly noise and the wrong voices get in the way. So discernment requires

- prayerful listening
- validation by others
- realistic assessment of your natural talents and personality

> **?** What has been your experience of discernment and callings?

> **?** When have you discerned correctly? Did you ever get it wrong?

Paying attention

Jesus told us to "have ears to hear and eyes to see." The practice of paying attention is like a private, silent way of keeping your spiritual ears and eyes open.

Three steps can help you see how the Spirit moves in your life:

Awareness. Become open to the Spirit drawing you to—or away from—people and things. Notice when and how the Spirit whispers, or when a thing you read, hear, or see stirs something inside you.

Name it. The Spirit always illuminates, shines a light. Work on describing the truth, lesson, or wisdom that the Spirit brings.

Keep it. Spiritually speaking this is called Integration, or making it part of the way you roll.

Another way of describing this is "See. Judge. Act." See what the Spirit is trying to show you, evaluate it, and make it part of you. Paying attention is the spiritual habit or practice of doing all three.

> **?** What is the Spirit trying to show you?

> **?** How well do you See, Judge, Act?

> **?** Which gives you the most difficulty? Why?

Contemplation

Contemplation is a spiritual practice of getting unplugged long enough to plug in to the Spirit and listen to the Soul's Friend.

During contemplation you empty yourself of worries and thoughts. You go inward to allow yourself to go upward. While there is spiritual power in solitude, contemplation doesn't require you to be in a private or quiet place.

You can practice contemplation on a crowded bus, walking along a street on a Saturday, sitting in a coffee shop, or changing in a locker room.

The key to contemplation is making it a habit. Most people find a certain time of day or a certain place to practice this deep prayer until it becomes a habit.

? If you haven't done much contemplation so far, what might be a first step? It can be something small.

? If you have practiced contemplation, how can you make it more of a habit?

Honest conversation

The Spirit can speak to us from above, from within, and through other people. The practice of Honest Conversation means *moving to a deeper level of conversation sooner* with certain people. It's about discussing soulful things that are on someone's mind or in someone's heart.

On one hand, opening up and trusting someone can involve risks. We don't want to open up to just anyone, and we don't have to talk about our deepest, darkest secrets. Just the soulful stuff.

On the other hand, we need discipline and sensitivity to do some deep listening to the hearts and the shy souls of others.

It is surprising how often we discover the Spirit's guidance and wisdom as we hear ourselves verbalize our deepest thoughts, concerns, and hopes. Or hear the ones spoken by others.

Honest conversation can take place with the same person for a long period of time, but sometimes the Spirit gives us a surprising Honest Conversation with someone we rarely see. As always, the key to encountering the Spirit is to stay open.

? What's in your heart and on your mind that you want to talk about, or think out loud about?

"The More"

"There is more I have to tell you, but you cannot bear it now. But when he comes, the Spirit of truth, he will guide you to all truth. He will not speak on his own, but he will speak what he hears, and he will declare to you more things."

▶ JOHN 16:12–13

The Spirit wants to share more with you. Much more. That's what Jesus told his Apostles as he bid them farewell.

After confirmation, your whole life can be a journey of more… more illumination…more awakenings…more about the ways of God the Father, Son, and Holy Spirit.

There is More. Much More than what you have studied or discovered so far. Keep listening for it. Keep asking the Spirit to show you some More.

In the third book of the *Lincoln Park* trilogy, a young high school teacher is having a conversation with her mother Katherine, a person experienced in Spirit. Katherine tells her daughter to take the next step:

> "I mean take the Spirit step. There is Spirit in everything we do, and we are cooperating and resisting its invitations all the time. All I'm saying is bring it up. Don't be shy. It is the secret energy of what is happening to them. Don't let it stay a secret."
>
> "I'm not sure I can do that. I'm not trained for spiritual stuff. Didn't exactly go to school to learn how to do this, Mom!"
>
> "You've been in Spirit school all your life," Katherine said softly. "Spirit school has visible and invisible campuses. It has teachers everywhere—friends and strangers, familiar and unfamiliar situations, sights and sounds, the mysterious universe…and the small voice of the soul inside you. Spirit school is not a classroom in a building. Your life is the classroom of Spirit school. And you've been a good student, Jamie."
>
> "One question though," Jamie asked.
>
> "What?"
>
> "When do you graduate from Spirit school?"
>
> "It's not about graduating," Katherine smiled. "It's about always staying in school."
>
> » Excerpted from *Lincoln Park: Original Soul*, by John Shea and Mike Carotta, Harcourt Religion Publishers

Katherine's words are true for each of us, as we stay open for More of the Spirit, as Jesus promised. Here are some ways to help you remain open to the More. Remember that:

- Spiritual growth involves *thinking* and *doing*.

- To discover the More, the Spirit asks you to see past the physical and the social.

- The Spiritual life requires discipline.

- Sometimes tests are given to see how you're doing.

- You move within a communion of saints, so keep an open mind.

- You are not meant to travel this path alone, that's why Christ established the Church. That's why the Holy Spirit descended on the Church at Pentecost.

- Seeking the More involves the authentic Pursuit of Truth. To pursue Truth, you must become familiar with the Bible and the teachings and Tradition of the Church. It's okay to pursue the core truth about yourself too.

- You need reminders: slogans, objects, songs, places, memories, rituals, traditions, and stories to keep going.

- The Spirit illuminates the mind, gladdens the heart, and activates the will. Look for all three whenever you think you are inspired.

- You have to pray always and all ways. Keeping the Lord's Day and Eucharist are critical for sustaining the Spirit and discovering the More. Nothing trumps these two forms of prayer.